100% Vegetarian

THAI Cooking

TARLA DALAL
India's # 1 cookery author

S&C

Eighth Printing : 2007

ISBN 10 : 81-86469-42-7
ISBN 13 : 978-8-186469-42-2

Price **Rs. 230/-**

Published & Distributed by : Sanjay & Company

353/A-1, Shah & Nahar Industrial Estate, Dhanraj Mill Compound,
Lower Parel (W), Mumbai - 400 013. INDIA.
Tel. : (91-22) 2496 8068 ● Fax : (91-22) 2496 5876 ● E-mail : sanjay@tarladalal.com

: Research Team :	: Designed by :	: Food Stylist :	: Production Designers :	: Photography :
Pinky Chandan	S. Kishor	Nitin Tandon	Lorella Jacinto	Vinay Mahidhar
Arti Kamat			Preeti Braganza	
Prasad Lele				

UK and USA customers can call us on :
UK : 02080029533 ● USA : 213-634-1406
For books, Membership on **tarladalal.com**, Subscription for **Cooking & More** and Recipe queries
Timing : 9.30 a.m. to 7.00 p.m. (IST), from Monday to Saturday
Local call charges applicable

OTHER BOOKS BY TARLA DALAL

INDIAN COOKING
Tava Cooking
Rotis & Subzis
Desi Khana
The Complete Gujarati Cook Book
Mithai
Chaat
Achaar aur Parathe
The Rajasthani Cookbook
Swadisht Subzian
Punjabi Khana New
Mughlai Khana New

WESTERN COOKING
The Complete Italian Cookbook
The Chocolate Cookbook
Eggless Desserts
Mocktails & Snacks
Soups & Salads
Mexican Cooking
Chinese Cooking
Easy Chinese Cooking
Sizzlers & Barbeques

MINI SERIES
Cooking Under 10 minutes
Pizzas and Pasta
Fun Food for Children
Roz ka Khana
Idlis & Dosas
Microwave - Desi Khana
Paneer
Parathas
Chawal
Dals
Sandwiches
Quick Cooking
Curries & Kadhis
Chinese Recipes

Jain Desi Khana
7 Dinner Menus
Jain International Recipes
Punjabi Subzis
Chips & dips
Corn
Microwave Subzis
Baked Dishes
Stir-Fry
Potatoes
Recipes Using Leftovers
Noodles New
Lebenese New

TOTAL HEALTH
Low Calorie Healthy Cooking
Pregnancy Cookbook
Baby and Toddler Cookbook
Cooking with 1 Teaspoon of Oil
Home Remedies
Delicious Diabetic Recipes
Fast Foods Made Healthy
Healthy Soups & Salads
Healthy Breakfast
Calcium Rich Recipes
Healthy Heart Cook Book
Forever Young Diet
Healthy Snacks
Iron Rich Recipes
Healthy Juices

Low Cholesterol Recipes
Good Food for Diabetes
Healthy Subzis
Healthy Snacks for Kids
High Blood Pressure Cook Book
Low Calorie Sweets
Nutritious Recipes for Pregnancy
Diabetic Snacks
Zero Oil Rotis & Subzis
Zero Oil Soups, Salads & Snacks
Zero Oil Dal & Chawal
Acidity Cook Book
Growing Kids Cookbook New
Soya Rotis & Subzis New

GENERAL COOKING
Exciting Vegetarian Cooking
Microwave Recipes
Saatvik Khana
The Pleasures of Vegetarian Cooking
The Delights of Vegetarian Cooking
The Joys of Vegetarian Cooking
Cooking with Kids
Snacks Under 10 Minutes
Ice-Cream & Frozen Desserts
Desserts Under 10 Minutes
Entertaining
Microwave Snacks & Desserts

Thai cuisine is an interesting confluence of flavours and cooking styles. Thailand has been influenced in its past by Chinese ,Malay and Indian cuisines. The Thais have skillfully adopted and adapted various techniques and made them their own.

In this book, we have endeavoured towards creating and adapting VEGETARIAN THAI MEALS. All the recipes have been selected keeping in mind locally available ingredients without compromising on the authenticity of each dish.

The most frequently used flavouring ingredients are lemon grass, chillies, ginger, soya sauce, limes and sugar. These ingredients represent sweet, salty, hot and sour flavours all of which are delicately balanced to maintain perfect harmony in each dish.
You can of course adjust the flavours to suit your personal preferences.

Rice is the heart of any Thai meal and is accompanied by a wide selection of different dishes , all of which are chosen to complement each other to achieve a perfect balance of flavours and textures. Steamed rice is a must on every Thai menu.

Many of the rice and noodle recipes in this book make great one dish meals needing no other accompaniment except a salad to refresh the palate.

It is also a very nutritious cuisine as most of the dishes are quickly cooked so as to preserve the nutrients.. For best results, use only the freshest available ingredients.

Do not let the long list of ingredients discourage you as much of the preparation is surprisingly quick and easy. Always keep all the ingredients measured and prepared before you start the actual cooking.

It is advisable to make 1 to 2 recipes of the curry pastes in advance and keep them refrigerated in air tight containers.

The Thais believe that food must please the eye as well as the taste buds and take great care in the presentation of dishes. They have made fruit and vegetable carving an art by skilfully creating flowers out of even chillies among other things.

There are no rigid rules in serving a Thai meal. Soup and starters can be served first or can be a part of the main meal along with the rice noodles and vegetables.

At the end of a meal, most Thais usually eat only fresh fruit which is artistically carved elevating a simple dish to a delicacy. Desserts are for more formal or special occasions.

Most of the desserts featured in this book are simple and easy to make, yet sumptuous.

Tarla Dalal

LEMON GRASS

Most commonly known in India as ' hari chai ki patti' or green tea leaves. It has a fragrant lemony smell that is most potent in its roots. In Thai cooking, usually only 10 cms. closest to the root are used, as the top can be slightly chewy if used in curry pastes. The top greens can however be used to flavour stocks and soups where the lemon grass can be removed before serving.

BASIL

Basil belongs to the 'tulsi' family. Basil is available in dried form or as fresh basil leaves which are packed and sold at some vegetable vendors. However, if you cannot find basil, use larger "tulsi" leaves. If you use dried basil, use only half the quantity specified in the recipe, as dried herbs are more concentrated .

MINT

Mint is also known as 'Pudina' and is easily available.

COCONUT CREAM and MILK

It is the liquid extracted from coconut flesh.

Coconut cream is the liquid extracted from the first pressing. It is the thickest and most concentrated extract.

Coconut milk is the product of the second and third pressing and is much thinner. Coconut milk is used in curries, while coconut cream is used mainly in desserts .

Coconut cream is available in cans and can be diluted with water to make coconut milk.

If you use coconut milk powder which is available at some shops, use 2 tablespoons in 1 cup of water to make coconut milk or 4 tablespoons in 1 cup of water to make coconut cream.

The recipe at the end of this book is very easy to follow.

BEAN SPROUTS

Beans sprouts are crisp shoots of the moong bean. These can be made at home by soaking moong beans in water overnight and then draining and tying them in a muslin cloth for 2 days till they germinate. They are a crisp addition to salads and stir-fries.

BROCCOLI

Broccoli is a vegetable from the cauliflower family. It looks similar to the cauliflower, but is green in colour and is available at selected vegetable vendors. Cauliflower is a good substitute for broccoli.

YELLOW AND RED PEPPERS

These are coloured variations of our local capsicum and are known as 'peppers' in some parts of the world. Red and yellow peppers are milder in flavour than their green counterpart. These are available at a few vegetable vendors. You can use green capsicum wherever yellow and red peppers are used.

BABY CORN

It is a miniature version of whole corn. It is very tender and all of it can be eaten, either stir-fried or parboiled if added in soups or curries.

MUSHROOMS

Thai cooking uses many different varieties of mushrooms. Since only a limited variety of mushrooms is available in India, button mushrooms have been used in most of the recipes. These are available both fresh and canned. It is important to drain and wash canned mushrooms under running water before using them. Likewise, when using fresh mushrooms, gently scrub them in water before cooking them.

DRIED CHINESE MUSHROOMS

These are available in packets at most grocers. They need to be soaked in hot water for 20 to 30 minutes, then washed and drained before use. These impart a unique flavour to the dishes in which they are used.

GINGER

'Galangal' ginger is most commonly used in Thai cooking. The Thais use a wide variety of different 'gingers' in their cooking, all of which have subtle differences. As we do not have all the varieties in India, very young or fresh ginger has been used as it has a milder flavour. A good indication of young ginger is that the skin should be thin, soft and pale in colour.

CORIANDER

Although we are familiar with coriander in India, Thai cooking uses the whole coriander plant including the stem and roots. Scrub the roots under running water before using them.

LEMON \ LIME RIND

This is the outer peel of the lemon \ lime that is yellow in colour. It is usually used in grated form. Using a fine grater, gently rub the fruit over, taking care to avoid the white layer under the skin as this imparts a bitter flavour to the food. As lime is not commonly available in India, lemon can be used.

SEASONING CUBE

This is made of salt and artificial flavours and seasonings. It is easily available at all grocery stores and is an alternative to making stocks for soups. Use 1 cube diluted in about 4 cups of water.

RICE NOODLES

Dried rice vermicelli noodles have been used as they are easily available in India and are the closest we can get to the Thai variety of rice noodles. Preparation of these noodles is included in the last portion of this book.

TOFU

Tofu or 'Bean Curd' as it is commonly known , is a product of soyabeans. As Tofu is not widely available in India, a basic recipe is given at the end of this book for those who would like to make it at home. Since its texture is quite similar to that of paneer, you can use paneer wherever Tofu is used.

BROWN SUGAR (DEMERARA SUGAR)

Although the Thai use Palm Sugar in their cooking, brown sugar (which is easily available at most grocers) imparts almost the same flavour to the food is used instead.

SHALLOTS

These are smaller onions, lighter in colour and milder in flavour and belong to the onion family.

SOUPS

STARTERS AND DIPS

SALADS

RICE

NOODLES

VEGETABLES

TABLE-TOP THAI COOKING

DESSERTS

BASIC RECIPES

SOUPS

HOT AND SOUR SOUP
Picture on page 17

A 'fat free' spicy aromatic soup, flavoured with lemon grass and simmered with mushrooms and baby corn.

Preparation time: 15 min.   Cooking time: 30 min.   Serves 4.

1 seasoning cube (vegetarian)
7 cloves garlic
50 mm. (2") piece ginger, cut into thin strips
5 stalks lemon grass, tied
¼ cup chopped coriander
3 green chillies, slit
3 tablespoons sliced canned mushrooms
7 to 8 nos. baby corn, cut diagonally
1 teaspoon lemon juice
salt to taste

For the garnish
2 tablespoons spring onions, finely cut
2 tablespoons chopped coriander
2 tablespoons carrots, cut into thin strips

1. Tie the lemon grass stalks and coriander together using some lemon grass.
2. Boil 5 cups of water in a pan. Add the seasoning cube, garlic, ginger, lemon grass and coriander (tied together), cover and simmer for 15 minutes.
3. When the aroma starts getting released, discard the garlic, ginger, lemon grass and coriander bunch.
4. Add the chillies, mushrooms, baby corn and salt and simmer for another 15 minutes in the covered pan.
5. Add the lemon juice just before serving.
6. Garnish the soup bowls with spring onions, coriander and carrot, pour the hot soup over it and serve at once.

☼Keep in mind that seasoning cubes already contain salt. Therefore, extra salt should be added last, if required.
☼Pouring hot soup over the spring onions, carrots and coriander helps release their flavours besides cooking them slightly.

SPICY COCONUT CREAM SOUP

A creamy coconut soup flavoured with Thai curry paste and served topped with fried onions.

Preparation time: 15 min.   Cooking time: 10 min.   Serves 4.

3 cups coconut milk, page 96
1 teaspoon cornflour
2 stalks lemon grass, tied into a bundle
1 teaspoon lemon juice
1 tablespoon soya sauce
½ cup mixed vegetables (peas, mushroom, broccoli, baby corn), blanched
1 teaspoon sugar
1 teaspoon oil
salt and pepper to taste

For the paste
1 dried red chilli
1 small onion, cut into slices
1 clove garlic, crushed
1 teaspoon ginger, grated
1 teaspoon oil

For the garnish
fried sliced onions

For the paste
1. Heat the oil in a small pan and fry the red chilli till it is crisp. Drain and keep aside.
2. In the same oil, fry the onion till light brown. Cool.
3. Make a paste of the garlic, ginger, red chilli and fried onion in a blender. Keep aside.

How to proceed
1. Mix the cornflour with the coconut milk.
2. Heat the oil in a vessel and add the coconut milk and cornflour mix, lemon grass, lemon juice, soya sauce, vegetables, sugar, salt and pepper.
3. Add the paste when the soup starts to simmer.

4. Add enough water to adjust the consistency.
5. Simmer for a few minutes.
6. Remove the lemon grass before serving.

Serve hot garnished with fried sliced onions.

☀Gently simmer this soup, constantly stirring it. Do not allow it to boil
since this could curdle the coconut milk.

SAGO SOUP

A thick sago soup flavoured with soya and lemon grass and
cooked with carrots and onions.

Preparation time: 10 min.   Cooking time: 10 min.   Serves 4.

1 seasoning cube (vegetarian)
2 tablespoons sago (sabu dana)
1 small onion, sliced into thin strips
1 carrot, cut into thin strips
1 teaspoon soya sauce
1 teaspoon lemon juice
½ teaspoon sugar
¼ teaspoon pepper powder
salt to taste

For the garnish
1 spring onion, finely chopped into rings·
1 teaspoon chopped coriander

1. In 4 cups of water, mix the seasoning cube and sago. Simmer for 5
   to 7 minutes till the sago is tender.
2. Add the onion and carrot and simmer again for 3 to 4 minutes.
3. Add the soya sauce, lemon juice, sugar, pepper powder and salt.

Serve hot garnished with spring onions and coriander.

☀You can use 4 cups of vegetable stock instead of the seasoning cube
and water.
☀This is a wonderful soup when the soya sauce, lemon juice and
sugar are well balanced.

POTATO AND SPRING ONION SOUP

Potatoes and spring onions simmered with carrots, mushrooms, basil and spices.

Preparation time : 10 min.   Cooking time : 10 min.   Serves 4.

1 seasoning cube (vegetarian)
2 to 3 peeled potatoes, cut into 25 mm. (1") cubes
1 large carrot, cut into slices
1 teaspoon cornflour
3 small spring onions, finely chopped into rings
2 dried Chinese mushrooms, soaked, drained and
     finely chopped (optional)
2 pinches chilli powder
1 teaspoon sugar
1½ teaspoons soya sauce
2 teaspoons lemon juice
2 small red or green chillies, slightly crushed
10 basil leaves
2 pinches pepper
salt to taste

For the garnish
1 teaspoon chopped coriander

1. Boil 4 cups of water with the seasoning cube, potatoes and carrot and then simmer for 5 to 7 minutes until the vegetables are soft.
2. Mix the cornflour in a little water and add to the soup. Simmer for a few minutes.
3. Add the spring onions, Chinese mushrooms, chilli powder, sugar, soya sauce, lemon juice, chillies, basil leaves, pepper and salt and simmer for a few minutes.

Serve hot and garnished with coriander.

☀This soup should be ideally cooked in a vessel with a lid on since that helps to draw out the flavours from the vegetables.

WHITE BEAN CURD SOUP

A simple but spicy soup cooked 'fat free'.

Preparation time: 10 min.   Cooking time: 10 min.   Serves 4.

1 seasoning cube (vegetarian)
1 cup tofu or paneer, page 93/94, cut into small cubes
1 tablespoon soya sauce
½ teaspoon sugar
½ teaspoon white pepper powder
2 spring onions, chopped
salt to taste

For the garnish
1 teaspoon chopped coriander

1. Boil 4 cups of water with the seasoning cube.
2. Add the soya sauce, sugar, pepper powder, spring onions and salt and simmer for 2 to 3 minutes.
3. Just before serving, add the tofu and simmer for 2 minutes.

Serve garnished with coriander.

☺Since seasoning cubes already contain salt in excess, you may not need to add any more salt to this recipe.
☺Instead of the seasoning cube and water, you can use 4 cups of freshly made vegetables stock, page 92.

1. Hot & Sour Soup, page 12.
2. Bean Sprout Yam, page 42.

THAI STYLE PUMPKIN SOUP

Picture on page 18

A delicious red pumpkin soup, mildly spiced with
Thai red curry paste.

Preparation time: 15 min.   Cooking time: 25 min.   Serves 4 to 6.

3 cups red pumpkin, peeled and cut into 12 mm. (½") cubes
1 onion, chopped
1 tablespoon red curry paste, page 94
2 cups coconut milk, page 96
1 seasoning cube (vegetarian)
1 tablespoon oil
salt to taste

For garnish

chopped coriander

1. Heat the oil in a large pot, add the onion and fry for a few minutes.
2. Add the red curry paste and fry for 4 minutes.
3. Stir in the pumpkin pieces, coconut milk and seasoning cube and
   2 cups of water.
4. Cover with a lid and simmer for 15 to 20 minutes or until the pumpkin
   is tender. Do not overcook.
5. Purée half the soup and leave the other half as it is. Add salt.
6. Mix both these, heat and serve garnished with coriander.

☀ If you would prefer a thick soup, purée all the ingredients.

1. Thai Style Pumpkin Soup, page 19.
2. Crispy Noodles, page 62.
3. Papaya Salad, page 45.
4. Massaman Curried Rice, page 56.

CHILLI FLOWERS

1. Slit the chilli lengthwise into thin strips.

2. Immerse in ice-cold water for 20 minutes till the strips curl.

SPRING ONION TASSELS

1. Slit the green portion of the spring onion into thin strips.

2. Immerse in ice-cold water for 20 minutes till the strips curl.

STARTERS & DIPS

CUCUMBER RELISH

Picture on page 35

A tangy cucumber relish which could be served with most Thai starters.

Preparation time: 10 min.   No cooking.   Makes 1 cup.

1 medium cucumber, peeled and chopped finely
1 small tomato, peeled and chopped finely
1 small red chilli, chopped finely
1 tablespoon vinegar
1½ tablespoons castor sugar
½ teaspoon salt

1. Combine the cucumber, tomato, red chilli, vinegar, castor sugar and salt in a bowl and mix well.
2. Keep aside for at least 2 hours before serving.

☺Make the relish a day in advance as the flavours mellow down and blend well.

HOT AND SWEET DIP

Picture on page 35

A traditional Thai dip flavoured wth crushed red chilli and sugar.

Preparation time: 5 min.   Cooking time: 10 min.   Makes 1½ cups.

2 tablespoons vinegar
¾ cup sugar
½ cup water
1 tablespoon red chilli flakes
1 tablespoon salt

1. Combine the vinegar, Sugar and water in a pan and boil till the mixture becomes a thick syrup.
2. Cool slightly, add the crushed red chillies and the salt.
3. Allow to stand for at least 6 hours before using.

☺Adjust the vinegar and chillies to your taste.

PEANUT SAUCE

A spicy sweet peanut dip flavoured with lemon grass and coconut.

Preparation time: 10 min. Cooking time: 15 min. Makes 1½ cups.

2 tablespoons peanut butter
1 tablespoon brown sugar
½ cup coconut milk, page 96
rind of ½ lemon
1 stalk lemon grass
½ red chilli, deseeded and finely chopped
½ onion, finely chopped
1 clove garlic, chopped
1 teaspoon oil
salt to taste

1. Heat the oil in a pan and fry the onion and garlic for 2 minutes.
2. Stir in the rest of the ingredients with ½ cup of water and simmer for 15 minutes.
3. Cool and remove the lemon grass before serving.

☺ If peanut butter is not available, you can use 2 tablespoons of peanut powder mixed in 1 tablespoon of oil.

SWEET AND SOUR DIP

Picture on page 35
Combine this sweet and tangy dip with any deep-fried Thai starter.

Preparation time: 10 min. Cooking time: 15 min. Makes 1½ cups.

100 ml. fresh tamarind pulp
200 grams jaggery, crumbled
2 teaspoons red chilli powder
2 tablespoons honey
½ cup water
1 teaspoon salt

1. Combine all the ingredients except the honey in a pan and simmer till the sauce reduces to half.
2. Cool and add the honey and salt. Mix well.

FRIED BEAN CURD WITH HOT AND SWEET DIP

Picture on page 35
A quick starter.

Preparation time: 10 min.   Cooking time: 15 min.   Serves 4.

4 cups tofu or paneer, page 93/94
hot and sweet dip, page 22

1. Slice the tofu in half diagonally.
2. Deep fry until it is golden brown.
3. Drain, arrange on a serving dish and serve with the hot and sweet dip.

☺ You can serve this with another dip of your choice.
☺ You can cut the tofu into fancy shapes using cookie cutters.

SWEET CORN CAKES

Picture on page 35

A crispy deep-fried corn starter flavoured with
Thai curry paste and soya sauce.

**Preparation time : 10 min.   Cooking time : 20 min.
Makes 18 to 20 cakes.**

2 cups tender raw sweet corn kernels
2 tablespoons red curry paste, page 94
1 tablespoon soya sauce
4 to 5 tablespoons rice flour
salt to taste
oil for deep frying

1. Lightly crush the sweet corn in a blender.
2. Add the red curry paste and soya sauce.
3. Bind this with the rice flour.
4. Using lightly oiled hands, form the batter into small patties and deep
   fry in hot oil.

Serve hot with a dip or relish of your choice.

⚙If sweet corn is not available, use regular corn.
⚙Adjust the amount of Thai curry paste to suit your taste.

FRIED BREAD AND YELLOW BEAN PASTE

Crispy starter of bread coated with a spiced yellow bean paste.

Preparation time: a few min.　　**Cooking time: 15 min.**　　**Serves 4 to 6.**

½ cup dried yellow moong dal, soaked for 30 minutes and drained
1 teaspoon chopped garlic
1 teaspoon whole black peppercorns
1 tablespoon soya sauce
1 teaspoon sugar
1 green chilli
1 tablespoon chopped coriander
½ cup potatoes, cooked and mashed
4 tablespoons cornflour
10 bread slices with crust removed
salt to taste
oil for deep frying

1. Mix the drained moong dal with the garlic, black peppercorns, soya sauce, sugar and green chilli.
2. Put in a food processor and make a smooth paste.
3. Remove in a bowl and mix in the coriander, mashed potatoes and cornflour to make a thick paste. Add salt.
4. Using a knife, spread a generous layer of this paste on the bread slices.
5. Deep fry in oil till golden brown.
6. Drain and cut each slice of bread into 4 triangles.

Serve hot with a sauce of your choice.

☼ The bean paste can be made well ahead of time and frozen till required.

GOLD BAGS

Picture on page 35

Dainty pouches filled with spicy vegetables and
tied with a blade of lemon grass.

**Preparation time: 30 min.   Cooking time: 10 min.
Makes 25 to 30 bags.**

For the wrappers

1½ cups plain flour (maida)
½ teaspoon salt

For the filling

1 teaspoon chopped garlic
1 teaspoon chopped coriander
½ teaspoon whole black peppercorns
1½ cups mashed potatoes
2 tablespoons carrots, grated
2 tablespoons roasted peanuts, ground
1 tablespoon soya sauce
½ teaspoon sugar
½ teaspoon salt

Other ingredients

1 tablespoon cornflour, mixed with water to make a paste
oil for deep frying

For the wrappers

1. Sieve the flour and salt together.
2. Add the hot water gradually and make a soft dough.
3. Knead for a while and keep aside for 30 minutes.
4. Apply oil on your palm and knead the dough until it becomes smooth
   and elastic.
5. Roll out thinly on a floured surface, using a rolling pin and cut into
   25 to 30 squares of 75 mm. (3").

For the filling

1. Pound the garlic, coriander and peppercorn in a mortar to
   form a paste.
2. In a bowl, mix the paste with the mashed potatoes, carrots, peanuts,
   soya sauce, sugar and salt. Mix thoroughly.

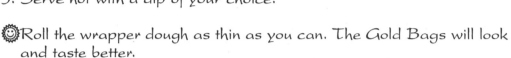

How to proceed
1. Place a spring roll sheet on a dry surface.
2. Fold the gold bags as illustrated in the diagram.
3. Deep fry in hot oil till golden brown.
4. Drain & tie with a blade of lemon grass.
5. Serve hot with a dip of your choice.

☺Roll the wrapper dough as thin as you can. The Gold Bags will look and taste better.

How to make a Gold Bag.
1. Spoon a little of the filling mixture in the centre of a wrapper square and gather all 4 corners in the centre to form a pouch.
2. Seal the centre of the fold with a little cornflour paste.
3. Fluff out gathers to make it look like a money bag.

2

MUSHROOM BALLS
A simple starter of batter fried mushrooms.

Preparation time: 10 min.   Cooking time: 15 min.   Serves 4 to 6.

3 cups button mushrooms
oil for deep frying

For the batter
1¼ cups plain flour (maida)
¼ cup cornflour
½ teaspoon white pepper powder
1 teaspoon sesame seeds
salt to taste

For the batter
Mix together the flour, cornflour, pepper, sesame seeds and salt with ½ cup of water to form a smooth batter. Set aside.

How to proceed
1. Wash, drain and dry the mushrooms.
2. Dip the mushrooms in the batter and deep fry till golden brown.

Serve hot with sweet and sour dip, page 23

✹ Make sure the prepared batter is thick enough to coat the mushrooms.

SWEET POTATO CAKES

Picture on page 35

Lightly spiced sweet potato croquettes flavoured with
toasted coconut and garlic and coated with sesame seeds.

Preparation time: 15 min.   Cooking time: 30 min.   Serves 4 to 6.

450 grams sweet potatoes
225 grams potatoes
2 tablespoons chopped coriander
50 grams desiccated coconut, toasted
1 tablespoon soya sauce
1 tablespoon lemon juce
1 tablespoon plain flour (maida), for your hands
1 teaspoon oil
6 cloves garlic
4 green chillies, chopped
50 grams sesame seeds
salt and pepper to taste
oil to shallow frying

1. Peel and boil the sweet potatoes and the potatoes. Cool.
2. Drain well and mash in a large bowl.
3. Heat the oil and fry the garlic and green chillies for a while. Add to
   the mashed potatoes.
4. Add the chopped coriander, toasted coconut, soya sauce,
   lemon juice, salt and pepper.
5. With lightly floured hands, form the mixture into small croquettes.
6. Dip the croquettes in sesame seeds and press firmly so that they
   stick on the surface.
7. Shallow fry in oil till golden brown.

Serve hot.

☀You can use only sweet potatoes and omit regular potatoes
   altogether.

SPRING ROLLS
Picture on page 35
The traditional Thai version of the famous Chinese spring roll.

**Preparation time: 15 min.   Cooking time: 20 min.
Makes 15 spring rolls.**

15 sheets of spring roll wrappers, page 27

For the filling
½ cup carrot, cut into strips
1 cup spinach leaves, shredded
½ cup rice vermicelli noodles, cooked and drained
2 green chillies, finely chopped
1 clove garlic, finely chopped
2 teaspoons soya sauce
1 tablespoon chopped coriander
1 teaspoon lemon juice
1 teaspoon oil
¼ teaspoon pepper
salt to taste
oil to deep frying

For the filling
1. Heat the oil in a wok, add the carrot and stir fry for 2 minutes.
2. Add the spinach and noodles, stir in the green chillies, garlic, soya sauce, coriander and lemon juice.
3. Add salt and pepper.
4. Cool and keep aside.

How to proceed

1. Place one wrapper on a dry surface.
2. Place a spoonful of the filling mixture in one corner of the wrapper.
3. Roll the wrapper over the filling, folding the sides as you go to form a small spring roll.
   Press the seams together with a little water and seal the edges.
4. Deep fry in hot oil till golden brown.

Serve hot with any sauce or relish of your choice.

☀ If you do not wish to use rice vermicelli, you can use bean sprouts or tofu in the filling.

How to make Spring Rolls

1. Place the filling mixture in one corner of the spring roll sheet.
2. Roll the wrapper over the filling carefully.
3. Fold the sides to seal all the edges.
4. Press the seams together with a little water.

Brush on some water.

PANEER, MUSHROOMS AND CAPSICUM SATAY

Picture on page 35

A very famous Far Eastern speciality. Paneer, mushrooms and capsicum skewers served with a peanut marinade.

Preparation time : 25 min.   Cooking time : 15 min.
Makes 6 skewers.

200 grams paneer, cut into 25 mm. (1") cubes
4 capsicums (green, yellow, red if available) cut into 25 mm. (1") cubes
12 large mushrooms

For the peanut sauce
½ onion, chopped
2 cloves garlic
2 tablespoons peanut butter
1 tablespoon brown sugar
½ cup coconut milk, page 96
1 stalk lemon grass
1 teaspoon chilli powder
rind of ½ lemon
juice of ½ lemon
1 teaspoon oil
salt to taste

For the peanut sauce
1. Heat the oil in a pan and fry the onion and garlic till soft. Add the remaining ingredients except the lemon juice and simmer for 10 to 15 minutes.
2. Turn off the heat, remove the lemon grass and add the lemon juice.
3. Cool and keep aside.

How to proceed
1. In a bowl, mix the sauce with the vegetables and the paneer carefully, so as not to break them.
2. Allow to stand for 15 to 20 minutes.
3. Put the vegetables and paneer alternately on six bamboo skewers.
4. Heat the oil on a tava and place the skewers on the tava. Grill on all sides till the vegetables brown lightly. Serve with extra sauce.

☻You can use any other vegetables of your choice.
☻You can also grill the satay on a barbecue grill.

CRISPY VEGETABLES

Fresh vegetables, dipped in a sesame seed batter,
deep fried to a golden brown.

Preparation time: 10 min.   Cooking time : 5 min.   Serves 4.

400 grams fresh vegetables
(capsicum, carrots, broccoli , cauliflower etc.)
oil for deep frying

For the batter

1 cup plain flour (maida)
½ cup cornflour
¼ teaspoon pepper powder
1 teaspoon sesame seeds
salt to taste

For the batter

Mix the flour, cornflour, pepper, sesame seeds and salt with enough
water to make a thick batter for coating vegetables.

How to proceed

1. Dip the vegetables in the batter and deep fry till golden brown.
2. Drain and serve with an assortment of relishes and dips.

☀ Use the freshest vegetables for best results.
☀ Ensure the the oil is very hot before frying the vegetables or
   otherwise you might end up with soggy fritters.

1. Paneer, Mushrooms and Capsicum Satay, page 33.
2. Cucumber Relish, page 22.
3. Hot and Sweet Dip, page 22.
4. Sweet and Sour Dip, page 23.
5. Gold Bags, page 27.
6. Spring Rolls, page 31.
7. Sweet Corn Cakes, page 25.
8. Sweet Potato Cakes, page 30.
9. Fried Bean Curd with Hot and Sweet Dip, page 24.

SALADS

SOUTHERN STYLE YAM

A warm salad of broccoli, long beans and beans sprouts in
a fiery chilli dressing with mushrooms and coconut cream.

Preparation time: 10 to 15 min. Cooking time: 15 min. Serves 4.

For the salad
½ cup bean sprouts
½ cup long beans (chawli), chopped
1 cup broccoli stalks

For the dressing
½ cup coconut milk, page 96
1 cup mushrooms, sliced
1 teaspoon red curry paste, page 94
2 tablespoons vegetable stock, page 92
a pinch turmeric powder
1 tablespoon soya sauce
1 tablespoon lemon juice
1 teaspoon sugar
1 tablespoon oil
salt to taste

For the garnish
1 tablespoon sesame seeds
2 small onions, finely chopped
1 teaspoon oil

For the salad
1. Blanch all the vegetables separately in salted water. Drain.
2. Pour cold water on top immediately to stop cooking and to retain the
   colour of the vegetables.
3. Arrange the vegetables decoratively on a serving platter & keep aside.

For the dressing
1. In a pan, pour the coconut milk, add the mushrooms and bring to a
   boil. Set aside.
2. In another pan, heat the oil, add the red curry paste and fry for a
   few minutes.
3. Add the vegetable stock, turmeric powder, soya sauce, lemon juice,
   sugar and salt.
4. Stir in the mushrooms cooked in the coconut milk.
5. Bring to a boil and keep aside.

For the garnish
1. Heat the oil in a pan and add the sesame seeds. When they crackle, add the onions and fry till they are light brown in colour.
2. Keep aside.

How to proceed
1. Pour the warm dressing over the platter containing the blanched vegetables.
2. Garnish with the fried onions and sesame seeds.

☺ Use any other vegetables if broccoli or sprouts are not available.

GREEN PAPAYA SALAD
Picture on page 36
A sweet and hot classic Thai salad of raw papaya, tomatoes and long beans in a nutty tamarind chilli dressing.

Preparation time: 15 to 20 min.   No cooking.   Serves 4 to 6.

3 cups raw papaya, thickly grated into long strips.
1 tomato, quartered and sliced thin
½ cup long beans (chawli), sliced finely
3 to 4 green chillies, pounded
½ cup roasted peanuts, crushed
3 tablespoons sugar
2 tablespoons lemon juice
2 tablespoons chopped coriander
salt to taste

1. Chill the grated papaya in iced water for 10-15 minutes. Just before serving toss the all ingredients together.
2. Serve chilled.

HOT & SOUR NOODLE-VEGETABLE SALAD

A colourful presentation of vegetable salad tossed in a spicy lemon-soya dressing.

Preparation time: 20 min.   Cooking time: 2 to 3 min.   Serves 4.

1 cup button mushrooms, blanched and sliced
1 cup boiled noodles, page 92
2 small onions, sliced
1 stalk celery with leaves, chopped
1 small carrot, finely chopped
50 grams broccoli florets, blanched
1 red capsicum, deseed and cut into slices

For the dressing
2 tablespoons lemon juice
1½ tablespoons soya sauce
½ teaspoon chilli powder
1 teaspoon sugar
1 clove garlic, finely chopped
1 teaspoon oil

For the garnish
4 to 5 crisp lettuce leaves
2 tablespoons chopped coriander

For the dressing
1. Heat the oil and fry the garlic till light brown. Cool.
2. Mix with all the other ingredients and keep aside.

How to proceed
1. Line a serving bowl with the lettuce leaves and keep aside.
2. In another bowl, mix all the ingredients, pour the dressing over and toss the salad.
3. Spoon the salad over the lettuce leaves and garnish with chopped coriander.

❀While blanching the broccoli and mushrooms, arrest their further cooking by placing them under running cold water.

LONG BEAN SALAD

A traditional Thai salad of pounded long beans in an Oriental dressing.

Preparation time: 20 min.   No cooking.   Serves 4.

1 bundle long beans (chawli), chopped
1 tomato, sliced
3 cloves garlic
1 small red chillies, deseeded
1 teaspoon soya sauce
2 tablespoons lemon juice
1 teaspoon sugar
1 tablespoons chopped peanuts
4 to 5 lettuce leaves
salt to taste

1. Pound the long beans lightly with a pestle.
2. In a mortar, crush the garlic and red chillies with the soya sauce, lemon juice and sugar.
3. Toss the long beans with the tomato and mix the dressing in it.
4. Make a bed of the lettuce leaves and serve the salad on it, topped with chopped peanuts.

☼Use extremely tender long beans.

BEAN SPROUT YAM
Picture on page 17
Fresh bean sprouts in a peanut chilli dressing.

Preparation time: 10 min.   Cooking time: 5 min.   Serves 4.

1½ cups bean sprouts
¼ red capsicum, sliced thin

For the dressing
1 garlic clove, crushed
1 tablespoon vinegar
1 tablespoon soya sauce
½ teaspoon sugar
½ teaspoon chilli powder
1 red chilli, finely sliced
2 tablespoon ground peanuts
1 tablespoon oil

For the garnish
1 spring onion, chopped
chopped coriander
strips of yellow and red pepper

For the dressing
1. In a pan, heat the oil and fry the garlic. Keep aside. Drain the oil.
2. Mix the garlic with the vinegar, soya sauce, sugar, chilli powder,
   red chilli and peanuts.

How to proceed
1. In a bowl, place the bean sprouts, capsicum and red chilli and pour
   the dressing over it.
2. Toss the salad.
3. Serve chilled garnished with spring onions, coriander,
   yellow and red peppers.

☺You can add cucumber or lettuce if you like.

CUCUMBER YAM

Fresh cucumber and tomatoes in a sweet sour
dressing with crunchy peanuts.

Preparation time: 10 min.   No cooking.   Serves 4.

4 cucumbers, peeled and cut into thin strips
2 medium tomatoes, cut into segments
2 tablespoons roasted peanuts, coarsely crushed

For the dressing
2 cloves garlic
2 small green chillies, chopped
1 teaspoon lemon juice
1 teaspoon soya sauce
2 teaspoons sugar

For the dressing
1. Pound the garlic and green chillies in a mortar.
2. Mix with the lemon juice, soya sauce and sugar.

How to proceed
1. Mix the cucumbers and tomatoes with the dressing and toss well.
2. Finally add the peanuts, turn once and refrigerate.
   Serve chilled.

☼ Instead of cutting it into strips, grate the cucumber using a large
   grater.

RED AND GREEN SALAD WITH PEANUT DRESSING

Picture on page 72

Red pepper, tomato and salad greens tossed together
in a lemon peanut dressing.

Preparation time: 20 min.   No cooking.   Serves 6.

3 sticks celery, diced
1 red pepper, diced
6 spring onions, chopped
1 medium cucumber, peeled and diced
3 tomatoes, diced
1 cup lettuce leaves, pak choy, spinach, shredded
1 yellow pepper, diced
6 spears asparagus
½ cup sliced carrots

To be mixed into a peanut dressing
4 tablespoons crushed peanuts
2 tablespoons chopped coriander
1 clove garlic, crushed
juice of 3 lemons
2 tablespoons sugar
1 tablespoon sesame seeds
salt to taste

1. Place the vegetables in a salad bowl and pour the dressing over.
2. Serve immediately.

PAPAYA SALAD
Picture on page 18
A Thai garden salad of papaya, cabbage, tomatoes and spring onions in an Oriental soya dressing.

Preparation time: 10 to 15 min.   No cooking.   Serves 4.

½ ripe papaya, peeled and sliced
1 cup shredded cabbage
2 spring onions
½ cup bean sprouts
1 tomato, sliced thin

For the dressing
1 green chilli
2 teaspoons sugar (approx.)
1 tablespoon soya sauce
1 teaspoon oil
1 tablespoon lemon juice
salt to taste

For the garnish
1 tablespoon ground peanuts
1 tablespoon chopped coriander

For the dressing
Pound the green chilli finely in a mortar. Add the sugar, soya sauce, oil and lemon juice. Adjust salt and sugar to your liking.

How to proceed
1. Mix the papaya, cabbage, onions, bean sprouts and tomato in a bowl.
2. Just before serving, pour the dressing over the salad. Garnish with the peanuts and coriander.

☺Serve the dressing separately and encourage your guests to pour as much as they like. For this, double the ingredients for the dressing as given in the recipe.
☺Use a firm ripe papaya for best results.

GLASS NOODLE SALAD

A sweet and spicy noodle and vegetable salad.

Preparation time: 20 min.   No cooking.   Serves 6 to 8.

2 cups rice noodles, page 92
2 cups tofu or paneer, page 93/94, cubed and fried
2 cups fresh mushrooms, sliced
1 onion, sliced
2 tomatoes, halved and sliced
1 celery stem, cut thin
3 tablespoons hot and sweet dip, page 22
salt to taste

Just before serving, toss all the ingredients together.

☺The best way to shred lettuce and spinach for salads is to tear the leaves with your hands.

RICE

GRILLED CURRY RICE

An aromatic rice preparation steamed in a banana leaf.

Preparation time: 15 min. Cooking time: 15 min. Serves 4.

3 cups cooked Basmati rice
½ cup coconut cream, page 96
1½ teaspoons red curry paste, page 94
2 tablespoons canned mushrooms, sliced (optional)
¼ cup green peas, boiled
4 nos. baby corn, blanched
10 french beans, sliced thin diagonally, cooked
½ teaspoon lemon rind, grated
1 tablespoon basil leaves, finely chopped
½ banana leaf
salt to taste

1. Mix the coconut cream and curry paste in a bowl.
2. Add the mushrooms, green peas, baby corn and french beans and stir well. Add the lemon rind, basil leaves and salt and mix well.
3. Add the rice, stirring until thoroughly mixed.
4. Turn this flavoured rice into the centre of a banana leaf (kitchen foil can be used as substitute).
5. Fold the leaf into a square packet and grill on a tava, turning around from time to time until steam comes out.

☀This recipe makes good use of left-over rice.

THAI LAYERED RICE

An innovative fruity vegetable rice cooked in coconut milk.

Preparation time: 15 min. Cooking time: 30 min. Serves 4.

For the rice
1 cup Basmati rice
1 cup coconut milk, page 96
1 teaspoon salt
4 tablespoons chopped coriander
1 tablespoon oil

For the vegetable curry
1 cup broccoli, cut into florets
8 to 10 nos. baby corn, sliced diagonally
2 tablespoons red curry paste, page 94
1 teaspoon cornflour
1 cup coconut milk, page 96
½ fresh pineapple, peeled, cored, cut into 25 mm. (1") cubes
2 tablespoons lemon juice
2 teaspoons sugar
1 tablespoon soya sauce
rind of 1 lemon, grated
2 tablespoons oil
salt to taste

For the garnish
2 tablespoons sliced onions, fried till brown
2 tablespoons spring onions, chopped

For the rice
1. Wash and drain the rice.
2. Heat the oil in a pan, add the rice and sauté for 4 to 5 minutes.
3. Add the coconut milk, 1 cup of water and the salt.
4. Bring to a boil, cover the pan with a lid and cook till the rice is done.
5. Sprinkle the coriander on top and keep aside.

For the vegetable curry

1. Blanch the broccoli and baby corn in hot water. Drain.
2. Heat the oil in a pan, add the red curry paste and fry for a few minutes.
3. Mix the cornflour in the coconut milk and add to the fried curry paste.
4. Add the blanched vegetables and the pineapple to the gravy.
5. Add the lemon juice, sugar, soya sauce, lemon rind and salt.
6. Bring to a boil and then keep aside.

How to proceed

1. In a flat bottomed pan, spread a layer of rice and top with a layer of the vegetable curry.
2. Repeat the layers till all the rice and vegetable curry are used.
3. Cover with a lid and seal the sides with a dough made of plain flour (maida) and water.
4. Bake in a preheated oven at 200°C (400°F) for 20 minutes.
5. Remove from the oven and break the seal.
6. Serve hot garnished with the brown onions and spring onions.

 To avoid the grains from breaking, fry the rice very gently.

GREEN RICE

Picture on page 54

Long-grain rice with green chilli, mint and coriander cooked in coconut milk. A perfect accompaniment for fiery Thai curry.

Preparation time: 10 min.   Cooking time: 15 min.   Serves 4 to 6.

2 cups Basmati rice, soaked for 1 hour
4 cups coconut milk, page 96
1 bay leaf
4 tablespoons chopped coriander
4 tablespoons fresh mint, chopped
4 green chillies, finely chopped
2 tablespoons oil
1 teaspoon salt

For the garnish
lemon wedges

1. Wash and drain the rice.
2. Heat the oil in a pan, add the rice and fry for 4 to 5 minutes.
3. Add the coconut milk, bay leaf and salt and cook on a slow flame with the lid on till all the liquid is absorbed.
4. Lower the heat as much as possible, cover the pan lightly and cook for 10 minutes more. Remove the bay leaf.
5. Stir in the coriander, mint and green chillies.
6. Serve hot garnished with lemon wedges.

☺ It is important to cook the rice on low heat as a high flame could cause the rice to stick to the bottom of the pan.

CHATUCHAK FRIED RICE

A Thai sweet-sour rice stir-fried with vegetables.

Preparation time: 15 min.   Cooking time: 5 to 7 min.   Serves 4.

2½ cups cooked rice
3 small onions, chopped
2 cloves garlic, crushed
1 teaspoon ginger, grated
1 red chilli, finely chopped
½ capsicum, sliced thin
¼ cup green peas, boiled
1 tomato, cut into 8 pieces
2 to 3 small brinjals, diced
1 cup bean sprouts
6 nos. baby corn, sliced thin diagonally
2 tablespoons tomato ketchup
2 tablespoons soya sauce
1 tablespoon oil
salt to taste

For the garnish
lemon wedges
chopped coriander

1. Heat the oil in a wok, add the onions, garlic, ginger and red chilli and fry for a few minutes.
2. Add the capsicum, peas, tomato, brinjals, baby corn and bean sprouts and cook till the brinjals soften.
3. Add the rice, ketchup, soya sauce and salt and mix well.

Serve hot, garnished with lemon wedges and coriander.

☀A good recipe which makes full use of left-over rice.

1. Coconut Ice-cream, page 86.
2. Thai Layered Jelly, page 88.

THAI FRIED RICE

Thailand's answer to the Chinese fried rice! Long-grained rice sautéed with baby corn, capsicum, spring onion and a hint of curry paste.

Preparation time: 10 min.   Cooking time: 5 min.   Serves 4.

3 cups cooked Basmati rice
4 to 6 nos. baby corn, sliced thin
1 large capsicum, sliced thin
2 tablespoons red or green curry paste, page 95
2 small red or green chillies, chopped
6 spring onions, chopped
2 tablespoons soya sauce
1 tablespoon oil
salt and pepper to taste

1. Heat the oil in a wok, add the baby corn and capsicum and stir fry for 2 to 3 minutes.
2. Add the curry paste, chillies and spring onions.
3. Add the rice, soya sauce, salt and pepper.

Serve hot.

☺You can change the quantity of curry paste to suit your taste.

1. Green Rice, page 51.
2. Thai Red Curry, page 70.
3. Thai Green Curry, page 68.
4. Tofu, page 93.
5. Coconut Milk, page 96.
6. Green Curry Paste, page 95.
7. Red Curry Paste, page 94.

MASSAMAN CURRIED RICE

Picture on page 18

This spicy stir-fried rice is a speciality of Muslim origin.

Preparation time: 15 min. Cooking time: 5 min. Serves 4.

For the massaman curry paste
1 teaspoon coriander seeds
1 teaspoon cumin seeds
1 teaspoon cloves
1 whole star anise
6 shallots, chopped
4 fresh red chillies, chopped
1 stalk lemon grass
rind of 1 lemon
1 teaspoon ground cinnamon
1 teaspoon oil
1 teaspoon salt

For the rice
4 cups cooked rice
1 cup tofu or paneer, page 93/94, cubed
¼ cup french beans, sliced thin, parboiled
¼ cup carrots, cut into thin strips, parboiled
1 tablespoon oil
salt to taste

For the garnish
6 spring onions, chopped
2 tablespoons crushed peanuts

For the massaman curry paste
1. Heat the oil in a pan, add the shallots, chillies and lemon grass and fry till the shallots soften. Cool and keep aside.
2. Dry roast the coriander seeds, cumin seeds, cloves and star anise. Cool.
3. In a blender, grind all the ingredients including the lemon rind, cinnamon powder and salt to a paste. Keep aside.

For the rice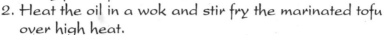

1. Marinate the tofu in some of the curry paste for 5 minutes.
2. Heat the oil in a wok and stir fry the marinated tofu over high heat.
3. Add the massaman curry paste with the french beans and carrots and fry for a few minutes.
4. Add the rice and salt and mix well.
5. Serve garnished with the spring onions and crushed peanuts.

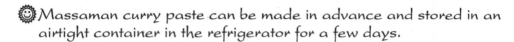 Massaman curry paste can be made in advance and stored in an airtight container in the refrigerator for a few days.

CUCUMBER FANS

1. Cut the cucumber into a 2" (50mm.)
long cylinder.
Cut the piece in half lengthwise.

2. Cut thin slices at the same angle,
taking care not to cut all
the way through.

3. Delicately turn the alternate
cucumber slices using your fingertip.

4. Leave in a bowl of ice water
for 2 to 3 hours.

RADISH DAISIES

1. Peel the radish and cut out
the marked design.

2. Cut out slices of
½ cm (5mm).

3. Decorate the centre with a
capsicum or a carrot circle.

NOODLES

THAI FRIED NOODLES

Picture on page 36

A very pleasing presentation of soft noodles and
bean curd combined with fresh vegetables and crunchy peanuts.

Preparation time: 10 min.   Cooking time : 10 min.   Serves 4.

3 cups rice noodles, page 92
1 cup tofu, page 93, cut into cubes and fried
4 spring onions, chopped
1 cup bean sprouts
2 tablespoons roasted peanuts, chopped
¾ teaspoon chilli powder
2 teaspoons sugar
2 tablespoons soya sauce
1 tablespoon lemon juice
2 cloves garlic, crushed
4 tablespoons oil
salt to taste

For the garnish
2 tablespoons chopped peanuts
1 tablespoon chopped coriander
1 lemon wedge

1. In a wok, heat the oil and add the crushed garlic.
2. Add the fried tofu, spring onions, bean sprouts,
   peanuts and noodles.
3. Add the chilli powder, sugar, soya sauce, lemon juice and salt.
4. Serve hot, garnished with the coriander and chopped peanuts.
5. Place the lemon wedge on the side of the plate.

☺ The fried vegetables need to remain sprightly and crisp.
☺ This dish should be prepared as close to serving time as possible as
   reheating it is not advisable.

NOODLES AND VEGETABLES IN CURRY SAUCE

A Thai variation of the popular Burmese Khowsuey.
Noodles and vegetables in a fiery Thai curry sauce.

Preparation time: 15 to 20 min.   Cooking time: 20 min.   Serves 4.

For the noodles and vegetables
1½ cups rice noodles, page 92
½ cup bean sprouts
½ cup long beans (chawli), cut into 25 mm. (1") pieces
¾ cup broccoli florets

For the curry sauce
1 cup coconut milk, page 96
1½ tablespoons red curry paste, page 94
1 teaspoon tamarind paste
1 teaspoon sugar
1 tablespoon roasted peanuts, chopped
1 small white onion, finely chopped
salt to taste

For the noodles and vegetables
1. Blanch the bean sprouts, long beans and broccoli florets in hot water for 2 to 3 minutes. Drain.
2. Place the noodles in the centre of a serving plate and arrange the blanched vegetables around the sides. Keep aside.

For the curry sauce
1. In a pan, mix the coconut milk and red curry paste. Add the tamarind paste, sugar, peanuts and onion and bring to a boil.
2. Add salt and simmer for a few minutes.

How to proceed
You can either pour the curry sauce over the noodles and vegetables or serve them separately.

✹ You could parboil the vegetables if you do not like them blanched.

CRISPY NOODLES
Picture on page 18
Deep fried noodles topped with a sweet and
sour caramelised onion sauce.

Preparation time: 10 min.   Cooking time: 15 min.   Serves 4.

60 grams raw rice noodles
1 cup tofu or paneer, page 93/94, cut into strips
oil for deep frying

For the sauce
2 cloves garlic, chopped
1 onion, sliced
1 tablespoon soya sauce
4 tablespoons sugar
1½ tablespoons lemon juice
½ cup vegetable stock, page 92
½ teaspoon chilli powder
2 tablespoons oil
salt to taste

For the garnish
½ cup red cabbage, diced
⅓ cup bean sprouts
1 spring onion, chopped
½ cup cauliflower florets
1 fresh red chilli, slit

1. Heat the oil and deep fry the raw noodles till golden. Drain and
   keep aside.
2. Deep fry the tofu till crisp. Drain and keep aside.

For the sauce
1. Heat the oil in a pan, add the garlic and onion and sauté till brown.
2. Add the soya sauce, sugar, lemon juice, stock and salt and stir till
   the mixture begins to caramelise.
3. Add the fried tofu, chilli powder and mix well.

MEE KROB

How to proceed
1. Pour over the fried noodles, just before serving.
2. Serve garnished with the red cabbage,
   bean sprouts and spring onion and cauliflower and
   top with the red chilli.

☺Pour the sauce over the noodles just before serving to avoid the crisp noodles from turning soggy.

DRUNKARD'S NOODLES
Stir-fried noodles flavoured with lemon rind and basil.

Preparation time: 15 min.   Cooking time: 20 min.   Serves 4.

2 cups rice noodles, page 92
2 cloves garlic, crushed
2 small red or green chillies, finely chopped
1 onion, sliced
1 tomato, quartered thin
rind of 2 lemons
6 basil leaves
2 teaspoons soya sauce
½ teaspoon sugar
2 green or red peppers, chopped
2 tablespoons oil
salt to taste

1. Heat the oil and add the garlic and chillies.
2. Add the noodles, onion, tomato, lemon rind, basil leaves, soya
   sauce, sugar, salt and peppers.
3. Stir well till the peppers soften slightly.

Serve immediately.

☺Grate only the yellow of the lemon rind, avoiding the white pith which gives a bitter after taste.

COCONUT RICE NOODLES

A colourful Thai preparation of noodles cooked with coconut cream and fresh vegetables.

**Preparation time: 15 min.   Cooking time : 10 to 15 min.
Serves 4 to 6.**

3 cups rice noodles, page 92
½ cup bean sprouts
1 tablespoon garlic paste
4 to 5 stalks celery, cut into 25 mm. (1") pieces
1 cup coconut cream, page 96
½ cup tofu or paneer, page 93/94, cubed
1 tomato, cut into wedges
1 green chilli, slit
2 spring onions, chopped
½ teaspoon chilli powder
2 teaspoons sugar
½ teaspoon pepper
1 tablespoon oil
salt to taste

For the garnish
1 tablespoon chopped coriander
1 tablespoon peanuts, chopped

1. Heat the oil in a wok, add the garlic paste and the celery stalks and stir for 1 minute.
2. Add the coconut cream, tofu, tomato, green chilli, spring onions, chilli powder, sugar, pepper and salt.
3. Stir and add the noodles.
4. Mix well and just before serving, add the bean sprouts and toss once.
5. Serve hot, garnished with the coriander and peanuts.

☼ It is not advisable to reheat this dish. Make it as close to serving time as possible.

THAI STIR-FRIED NOODLES WITH TOFU

Noodles, stir-fried with tofu and bean sprouts accompanied by a soya sauce.

Preparation time: 10 to 15 min.   Cooking time: 10 min.   Serves 4.

For the noodles
2 cups rice noodles, page 92
1 teaspoon ginger, grated
2 cloves garlic, chopped
1 cup tofu or paneer, page 93/94, cut into cubes
8 small onions, peeled and halved
1 tablespoon soya sauce
½ cup bean sprouts
1 teaspoon lemon juice
2 tablespoons roasted peanuts
1 tablespoon oil
salt to taste

For the sauce
2 to 3 tablespoons lemon juice
2 teaspoons soya sauce
4 tablespoons castor sugar
4 tablespoons peanut butter
salt to taste

For the noodles
1. Heat the oil in a wok, add the ginger, garlic, tofu, onions and soya sauce. Sauté these till the onion browns.
2. Add the noodles, bean sprouts, lemon juice and salt. Mix well.
3. Place on a serving dish and sprinkle chopped peanuts on top.

For the sauce
In a saucepan, combine all the ingredients with ½ cup of water and bring to a boil. Keep aside.

How to proceed
Serve the stir fried noodles and sauce side by side, so guests can pour as much sauce as they like over the noodles.

☺The sauce might need a little more water, so adjust the consistency as you go along.

RADISH AND CAPSICUM
PALM TREE

1. Peel and cut the radish from both ends.

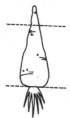

2. Using a sharp knife cut out a design so that it resembles a tree trunk.

3. Cut the lower 1/3 of the capsicum.

4. Using a scissors cut out thin strips.

5. Place the capsicum on the radish and fasten with a toothpick.

VEGETABLES

THAI GREEN CURRY

Picture on page 54

An aromatic green curry cooked with assorted
vegetables and paneer.

Preparation time: 10 min.   Cooking time 15 to 20 min.   Serves 4.

7 to 8 tablespoons green curry paste, page 95
2½ cups coconut milk, page 96
1 cup button mushrooms
½ cup green peas
1 cup cauliflower florets
1 capsicum, diced
1 cup baby corn, sliced
1 cup paneer, page 94, diced
1 teaspoon sugar
1 tablespoon oil
salt to taste

1. Parboil the mushrooms, peas, cauliflower, capsicum and baby corn.
2. Deep fry the paneer, drain and keep aside.
3. Heat the oil in a wok, add the green curry paste and
   fry for 2 minutes. Add the coconut milk.
4. Add the vegetables, paneer, sugar and salt and simmer for
   a few minutes.
5. Serve hot with steamed rice.

☺You can use any vegetables of your choice.

CURRY OF TOFU, MUSHROOMS AND VEGETABLES

A creamy spicy-sweet curry, cooked with bean curd, vegetables and mushrooms.

Preparation time: 20 min.   Cooking time: 20 min.   Serves 4 to 6.

To be ground to a paste
4 to 6 red chillies
¼ cup white onion, sliced
10 cloves garlic
½ teaspoon cumin seeds
2½ teaspoons coriander seeds
8 peppercorns
1 teaspoon ginger, grated
3 tablespoons coriander leaves
juice of 1 lemon
2 tablespoons brown sugar
1 teaspoon salt

Other ingredients
6 fresh mushrooms, big
½ cup green peas, boiled
½ cup carrot, cut into strips, boiled
½ cup french beans, cut thin, boiled
2 cups coconut milk, page 96
1 cup paneer or tofu, page 93/94, cubed
¼ cup basil leaves, chopped
1 tablespoon soya sauce
1 small bundle lemon grass, tied well
½ teaspoon lemon rind
juice of ½ lemon
2 tablespoons oil
salt to taste

1. Wash and boil the mushrooms in salted water and drain. Mix with the boiled vegetables.
2. Heat the oil in a pan and add the coconut milk and the paste. Stir well and cook for 4 to 5 minutes till it releases its flavours.
3. Add the mushrooms, vegetables, tofu, basil leaves, soya sauce, tied lemon grass, lemon rind, lemon juice and salt.
4. Simmer for 10 to 15 minutes till the lemon grass releases its juices.

5. Remove the lemon grass bundle.
6. Serve hot with steamed rice.

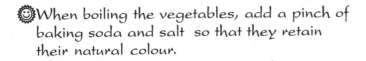☀When boiling the vegetables, add a pinch of
baking soda and salt so that they retain
their natural colour.

THAI RED CURRY
Picture on page 54
A traditional fiery red Thai curry simmered with
assorted vegetables. An excellent complement to steamed rice.

Preparation time: 10 min.   Cooking time: 15 min.   Serves 4 to 6.

6 to 7 tablespoons red curry paste, page 94
2 cups coconut milk, page 96
1 tablespoon cornflour, mixed in water
½ teaspoon soya sauce
15 basil leaves, chopped
½ cup baby corn, diced
2 brinjals, diced
1 cup broccoli florets
½ cup mushrooms, sliced
1 tablespoon oil
salt to taste

1. Mix the cornflour and coconut milk.
2. Heat the oil in a large pan, add the red curry paste and fry for
   a few minutes.
3. Add the coconut milk, soya sauce, basil leaves and
   all the vegetables.
4. Simmer for 10 minutes till the vegetables are tender.
5. Add salt.
6. Boil for 1 to 2 minutes till the curry thickens.

Serve hot with steamed rice or noodles.

☀You can use any vegetables of your choice.

1. Fresh Fruits With Coconut Cream Sauce, page 89.
2. Thai-Style Bananas , page 82.

G A N G ● P E D ● P A K

FRIED POTATOES WITH GINGER MUSHROOM SAUCE

Potato slices, fried golden brown and topped with a rich ginger mushroom sauce.

Preparation time: 15 min.   Cooking time: 25 min.   Serves 4.

3 large potatoes
oil to deep frying

For the ginger mushroom sauce
2 teaspoons cornflour
1 onion, chopped
1 teaspoon garlic, chopped
1 tablespoon ginger, cut into thin strips
½ cup dried mushrooms, soaked and chopped
1½ capsicums, cut into strips
2 spring onions, chopped
2 green chillies, chopped
1 tablespoons soya sauce
1 teaspoon sugar
½ cup vegetable stock, page 92
1 tablespoon oil
salt to taste

For the garnish
chopped coriander

1. Slice the potatoes into 6mm. (1/4") thick slices, without peeling them.
2. Deep fry the potato slices in oil.
3. Drain and keep aside on a serving dish.

For the sauce
1. Make a paste of the cornflour with 2 tablespoons of water and keep aside.
2. Heat the oil in a wok, fry the onion and garlic and sauté for a few minutes.
3. Add the ginger, mushrooms, capsicum, spring onions, green chillies, soya sauce, sugar and salt.
4. Stir in the cornflour paste and mix with the stock.

< Facing page: Red and Green Salad with Peanut Dressing, page 44.

How to proceed
1. Pour the sauce over the potatoes.
2. Serve hot, garnished with chopped coriander.

☼Make this sauce as close to serving time as possible.

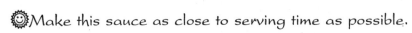

LEMON GRASS SPICY VEGETABLES

An aromatic stir-fried vegetables flavoured with lemon grass.

Preparation time: 15 min.   Cooking time: 10 min.   Serves 4.

2 red chillies, chopped
1 teaspoon ginger, grated
1 teaspoon garlic, chopped
2 small onions, chopped
¾ cup tofu or paneer, page 93/94, cut into cubes
½ cup broccoli florets
½ cup french beans, thinly sliced
½ cup carrots, thinly sliced
4 to 6 nos. baby corn, sliced diagonally
1 tablespoon grated coconut
1 tablespoon lemon grass, finely chopped
¼ cup water or vegetable stock, page 92
2 tablespoons soya sauce
1 tablespoon sugar
2 tablespoons oil
salt to taste

1. In a mortar or a blender, grind the red chillies, ginger, garlic and onions to a paste. Keep aside.
2. Deep fry the tofu. Drain and keep aside.
3. Parboil all the vegetables till tender and keep aside.
4. Heat the oil in a wok and fry the spice paste for 2 to 3 minutes.
5. Add the grated coconut and lemon grass and stir for a few minutes.
6. Add the water or stock, soya sauce, sugar and salt.
7. Stir in the vegetables with the tofu and mix well.
8. Serve hot with green rice, page...

☼Use only very tender lemon grass. The best way to finely chop lemon grass is to use a pair of scissors.

PEANUT SESAME VEGETABLES

Stir-fried vegetables in a tangy orange sauce with peanuts and sesame seeds.

Preparation time: 15 min.   Cooking time: 10 to 15 min.   Serves 4.

1 cup paneer, page 94, cut into strips
1 cup broccoli, divided into small florets
6 nos. baby corn, sliced diagonally
1 green capsicum, sliced
1 cup mushrooms, sliced
2 tablespoons soya sauce
1 cup orange juice
1 teaspoon cornflour
2 tablespoons roasted sesame seeds
2 tablespoons peanuts, roasted
3 tablespoons oil
salt and pepper to taste

To serve
rice or noodles

1. Heat the oil in a large pan or wok, add the paneer strips and fry till they are brown.
2. Add the broccoli, baby corn, capsicum and mushrooms and stir fry for 1 to 2 minutes.
3. Meanwhile, mix the soya sauce with the orange juice and cornflour and stir into the vegetables, stirring constantly till the sauce has thickened and a glaze develops.
4. Stir in the sesame seeds, peanuts, salt and pepper and cook for 3 to 4 minutes.

Serve hot with rice or noodles.

☀If you are using canned orange juice, dilute it with a little water.

PEPPERED MUSHROOMS, PANEER AND CASHEW

A colourful selection of vegetables stir-fried with cashew, paneer and pepper.

Preparation time: 20 min.   Cooking time: 10 min.   Serves 4.

1 onion, sliced
1 clove garlic, chopped
1 teaspoon ginger, grated
1 cup tofu or paneer, page 93/94, cut into cubes
1 cup mushrooms, sliced
2 teaspoons brown sugar
1 tablespoon soya sauce
1 red capsicum, sliced
1 green capsicum, sliced
1 yellow capsicum , sliced
4 spring onions, chopped
2 celery stalks, chopped
2 tablespoons cashewnuts
3 tablespoons vegetable stock, page 92
½ teaspoon pepper powder
2 tablespoons oil
salt to taste

1. Heat the oil in a pan, add the onion, garlic and ginger and sauté for 2 minutes.
2. Add the tofu, mushrooms, sugar and soya sauce. Mix well.
3. Toss in the capsicums, spring onions, celery and cashewnuts and mix well.
4. Add the stock, pepper powder and salt and stir till it is absorbed.

☻Stir-fry this dish as close to serving time as possible.

TABLE-TOP
THAI COOKING

STEAM BOAT SOUP

A light lemon grass flavoured soup, steaming on a burner surrounded by a selection of bowlfuls of flavourings and vegetables from which each guest can mix and match to prepare his own special soup.

Preparation time: 10 to 15 min.   Cooking time: 20 min.   Serves 6 to 8.

For the vegetable stock

2 litres water
6 peppercorns
2 onions, quartered
2 carrots, chopped
2 stalks lemon grass
salt to taste

Other ingredients

½ cup tofu or paneer, page 93/94, diced small
½ cup spring onions
½ cup sliced mushrooms
½ cup chopped coriander
½ cup spinach, shredded
½ cup baby corn, sliced, blanched
1 cup bean sprouts
1 small bowl chilli vinegar
10 flakes garlic (sautéed) in ½ cup of oil
½ cup soya sauce
chilli powder to taste

For the stock

1. In a pot, simmer all the ingredients till they release their flavours. This should take about 10 to 15 minutes.
2. Strain and keep aside.

How to proceed

1. Keep the vessel containing the soup on a burner, surrounded by bowls of the other ingredients.
2. Allow your guests to mix and match ingredients, adding as much as they like.

☼ Serve the soup piping hot.

TABLE-TOP THAI CURRY

A combination of vegetables in Thai red curry paste and green curry paste, cooked with a flourish right in front of your guests.

Preparation time: 30 min.   Cooking time: 5 min.   Serves 4.

For the vegetables

1 cup broccoli, cut into florets
1 cup cauliflower, cut into florets
1 cup baby corn, cut into two diagonally
1 cup mushrooms, cut into quarters
1 medium red pepper, cut into quarters
1 medium green pepper, cut into quarters
2 onions, sliced
1 cup coconut cream, page 96
1 teaspoon sugar
2 teaspoons oil
salt to taste

Other ingredients

red curry paste, page 94
green curry paste, page 95

For the garnish

6 spring onions, chopped
1 tablespoon chopped coriander

How to proceed

1. Boil each vegetable separately in salt water. Drain and keep aside.
2. In a flat pan, heat the oil, add the onions and fry for a few minutes.
3. Put 3 tablespoons of the red curry paste or green curry paste and sauté for some time.
4. Add the coconut cream and ½ cup of water and simmer for 2 minutes.
5. Add all the vegetables and stir thoroughly. Add the sugar and salt and mix.
6. Garnish with the coriander and spring onions.

☺ It is always advisable to have a slightly larger quantity of ingredients so as to ensure a trouble-free party.
☺ All seasonings and vegetables may be added as per your guest's individual preferences.

THAI PINEAPPLE RICE

Picture on page 36

Long-grained rice stir-fried with yellow curry paste, pineapple, raisins and cashewnuts. Served in a pineapple shell.

Preparation time: 25 min.   Cooking time: 20 min.   Serves 8.

1 fresh pineapple
6 cups cooked rice
1 cup coconut cream, page 96
3 onions, chopped
2 green chillies, chopped
2 tablespoons yellow curry paste, recipe below
4 tablespoons raisins
4 tablespoons cashewnuts, roasted
4 tablespoons butter
1 teaspoon sugar
salt to taste

For the yellow curry paste
1 tablespoon cumin seeds, roasted
1 tablespoon coriander seeds, roasted
2 stalks lemon grass, chopped
½ tablespoon ginger, grated
3 dried chillies, deseeded
2 cloves garlic
½ small onion, quartered
½ teaspoon turmeric powder
1 teaspoon salt

For the garnish
chopped coriander

For the yellow curry paste
Grind all the ingredients to a fine paste in a mortar or a food processor.

How to proceed
1. Cut the pineapple in half lengthwise , keeping the leaves on. Scoop out the flesh with a sharp knife to leave 2 shells with a thin border of flesh attached.
2. Chop the pineapple flesh and keep aside.

3. Heat the butter in a wok, add the onions and green chilli and fry till soft. Add the yellow curry paste and fry for 1 more minute.
4. Add the chopped pineapple.
5. Add the cooked rice, coconut cream, raisins and cashewnuts and stir till all the coconut cream has been absorbed.
   Add the sugar and salt.
6. Spoon the rice mixture into the empty pineapple shells.
7. Serve hot garnished with coriander.

☺ Use a fairly ripe pineapple so as to be able to scoop out the flesh easily.

THAI-STYLE BANANAS

Picture on page 71

A sweet lover's delight of warm caramelised bananas, sprinkled with sesame seeds and toasted coconut.

Preparation time: 10 min.   Cooking time: 15 min.   Serves 4 to 6.

For the orange zest
rind of 1 orange

Other ingredients
5 bananas
1 teaspoon ginger, grated
3 tablespoons powdered sugar
½ teaspoon lemon juice
3 tablespoons toasted grated coconut
3 tablespoons toasted sesame seeds
2 tablespoons brandy or orange liqueur (optional)
2 tablespoons butter

For the orange zest
1. Peel the orange and gently slice of all the white part out of the peel. Using a very sharp knife, chop the outer portion of the peel into fine pieces. Keep aside.

How to proceed
1. Peel and slice the bananas lengthwise and then halve them to get 4 pieces out of each.
2. In a flat pan, heat the butter.
3. Add the ginger and orange zest and cook over low heat till they release their flavours.
4. Add the bananas and powdered sugar and simmer till the syrup is thick, keep turning the bananas so they are well coated with the syrup.
5. Add the lemon juice.
6. Add the brandy or the orange liqueur and simmer till the syrup thickness.
7. Serve garnished with sesame seeds and toasted coconut.

☺This recipe tastes as good with apples or pears.
☺Serve with vanilla ice-cream.

DESSERTS

MANGO PANCAKES

Pancakes made from flour, grated coconut, mango pulp and cooked rice and filled with mangoes and fresh cream.

Preparation time: 10 min.   Cooking time: 20 min.   Serves 4 to 6.

For the pancakes
¾ cup plain flour (maida)
¾ cup powdered sugar
4 tablespoons shredded fresh coconut
2 mangoes, puréed
½ cup coconut milk, page 96
½ cup cooked and cooled rice
1 to 2 tablespoons oil

For the filling
1 mango, chopped
½ cup fresh cream
2 tablespoons powdered sugar

For the garnish
1 tablespoon castor sugar

For the pancakes
1. In a bowl, combine all the ingredients except the oil and make a smooth batter.
2. Heat a little oil in a non-stick pan, pour 1 tablespoon of the batter and spread evenly to make a circle.
3. Cook evenly on both sides till golden brown.
4. Repeat this process for the rest of the batter.

For the filling
1. Peel and chop the mango into small pieces.
2. Whip the cream with the powdered sugar till soft peaks form. Combine with the mango.

How to proceed
1. Spoon a little filling on each pancake and fold neatly into a semicircle.
2. Repeat with all the pancakes.

3. Arrange on a serving plate and sprinkle castor sugar over.
4. Serve immediately.

 If mangoes are not in season, use puréed bananas instead and adjust the sugar accordingly.

MANGO GINGER SORBET
A light summer-time mango sorbet flavoured with ginger and lime.

**Preparation time: 10 min.   Cooking time: 7 min.
Setting time: 7 hours.   Serves 4.**

2 large mangoes, peeled and puréed
1 teaspoon ginger, grated
4 tablespoons sugar
juice of 3 lemons
rind of 3 lemons

For the garnish
mint sprigs
mango slices

1. In a saucepan, combine the ginger and sugar with 1 cup of water and simmer for 5 to 7 minutes.
2. Allow to cool completely.
3. Add the lemon rind and juice to this syrup.
4. Add the mango pulp and mix well.
5. Transfer into a freezerproof container and freeze till slushy.
6. Remove from the freezer and beat till all the ice crystals are broken down.
7. Freeze again and repeat step 5 and 6.
8. About 15 minutes before serving, transfer the sorbet from the freezer to the refrigerator to soften a little.
9. Scoop out using an ice-cream scoop and serve immediately, garnished with mango slices and a sprig of mint.

If the mangoes are not sweet, omit the lemon juice and add enough sugar to taste at step 4.

COCONUT ICE-CREAM

Picture on page 53

A creamy coconut ice-cream.

Preparation time: 5 min. Cooking time: 10 min.
Setting time: 12 hours. Serves 4 to 6.

420 ml. coconut cream, page 96
4 tablespoons cornflour
1 cup castor sugar
280 ml. fresh cream
½ coconut, grated

1. Mix the cornflour in 2 to 3 tablespoons of cold water.
2. In a non-stick pan, bring the coconut cream to a boil and add the cornflour paste and stir till it coats the back of a spoon.
3. Remove from the heat and cool completely. Add the sugar and mix well.
4. Whip the cream till soft peaks form.
5. Combine the cooled coconut custard, grated coconut and fresh cream.
6. Pour into a shallow freezerproof dish and freeze till slushy.
7. Remove from the freezer and beat till smooth and creamy. Freeze again till firm.
8. Repeat step 7.
9. Remove from the freezer and place in the refrigerator for 20 minutes before serving.

☺ Set the ice-cream in aluminium containers so that it freezes quickly.
☺ Also make sure that the containers have lids to prevent the water within the ice-cream from crystallising.

THAI MANGO ICE-CREAM

A creamy mango coconut ice-cream, this combination is unique to Thailand.

Preparation time: a few min. **Cooking time: a few min.**
Setting time: 6 to 8 hours. **Serves 4 to 6.**

3 mangoes, peeled
420 ml. thick coconut cream, page 96
4 tablespoons custard powder
280 ml. fresh cream
8 tablespoons sugar

1. Mix the custard powder in 2 to 3 tablespoons of cold water and keep aside.
2. Heat the coconut cream in a heavy bottomed pan. When it comes to a boil, add the dissolved custard powder and sugar and stir till it coats the back of a spoon.
3. Remove from the heat and cool completely.
4. Chop half the mangoes into pieces and mash the other half to pulp.
5. Whip the cream till soft peaks form.
6. Mix the cooled custard with the cream and mangoes.
7. Pour into a shallow freezerproof dish and freeze till slushy.
8. Remove from the freezer and beat till smooth and creamy. Freeze again till firm.
9. Repeat step 8.
10. Remove from the freezer and place in the refrigerator for 20 minutes before serving.

☼Top with roasted flaked almonds.

THAI LAYERED JELLY

An extremely delicious and colourfully layered dessert flavoured with orange and coconut.

Preparation time: a few min.
Setting time: 4 to 5 hours.

Cooking time: 10 min.
Serves 4.

For the fruit layer
5 grams agar agar (China grass)
2 cups orange juice
sugar to sweeten
a few drops orange food colour

For the coconut layer
2 cups coconut milk, page 96
2 tablespoons cornflour
4 to 5 tablespoons sugar

For the fruit layer
1. Dissolve the agar agar in the orange juice till it softens.
2. Add the sugar and simmer till all the agar agar dissolves.
3. Strain while it is still warm and add the food colour.
4. Pour into a 150 mm. (6") square tray.
5. Refrigerate for 15 to 20 minutes till it sets.

For the coconut layer
1. Make a paste of the cornflour and 2 tablespoons of the coconut milk.
2. Heat the remaining coconut milk with the sugar.
3. When it comes to a boil, add the cornflour paste and stir till it becomes thick.
4. Remove from the fire, cool slightly and strain.
5. Pour this over the set orange layer and allow it to set in the refrigerator for 4 to 5 hours.

How to proceed
1. To unmould, place the tray in lukewarm water for a few seconds and unmould on a flat plate.
2. Using a flower shaped cookie cutter, cut out pieces from the set dessert.
3. Lift each piece carefully and place on a serving plate.
4. Serve chilled surrounded by fruit.

☀You can also use a layer of chocolate sponge as a base. (Picture on page 53)

FRESH FRUGTS WGTH COCONUT CREAM SAUCE

Picture on page 71

Fresh fruit topped with a coconut flavoured sauce.

Preparation time: 10 min.   Cooking time: 10 min.   Serves 6.

fresh seasonal fruits

For the coconut cream sauce

1 cup coconut cream, page 96
4 teaspoons cornflour
5 tablespoons sugar
2 tablespoons fresh cream
¼ teaspoon rose essence

For the coconut cream sauce

1. Dissolve the cornflour in 1 cup of water.
2. Heat the coconut cream with the sugar and when it comes to the boil, add the cornflour mixed with water.
3. Simmer for 1 minute and strain.
4. Cool completely.
5. Add the fresh cream and flavour with the rose essence.
6. Refrigerate till chilled.

How to proceed

1. Arrange the fruits in serving bowls.
2. Pour the coconut cream sauce on top of the fruit.
3. Serve chilled, garnished with mint leaves.

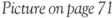Serve this on a bed of crushed ice.
You can use a melon scoop to get round balls of fruit.

FRUIT CARVINGS

MELON BASKET

1. Cut out 2 quarters from the top of the melon as directed.

2. Using a sharp knife scoop out the insides and decorate the edges by carving scallops.

3. Fill with fresh fruits or a salad and serve.

PAPAYA LEAVES
Picture on page 71

1. Cut the papaya into 4 parts vertically and remove the seeds.

2. Shape like a leaf using a sharp knife.

3. Carefully cut out thin veins.

BASIC RECIPES

VEGETABLE STOCK

**Preparation time: 10 to 15 min.   Cooking time: 25 min.
Makes 4 cups.**

1 medium onion, quartered
2 carrots, roughly chopped
2 stalks celery, roughly chopped
3 to 4 coriander stems
1 teaspoon whole peppercorns

1. Place all the ingredients in a large pan and add 6 cups of water.
2. Bring to a boil and then lower the heat.
3. Cover with a lid and simmer for 20 minutes till the vegetables have released their flavours.
4. Cool and strain.
5. Use as required.

☀Always start a stock in cold water and simmer gently so that the ingredients release their flavours.

RICE NOODLES

**Preparation time: 5 to 10 min. Cooking time : 5 to 10 min.
Makes 4 to 5 cups.**

200 grams rice noodles (dried rice vermicelli)
salt to taste
1 teaspoon oil

1. Place the noodles in a large bowl.
2. In another pan, boil about 2 litres of water with the salt and oil. When it comes to a boil, pour the water over the raw noodles. Cover and keep aside for 10 minutes or till the noodles are soft.
3. Drain and use as required.

☀The oil is added is prevent the noodles from sticking together.

TOFU

Picture on page 54

Tofu or soya bean curd is made from soya beans and is very high in protein content.

**Preparation time: 15 to 20 min.   Cooking time: 5 to 10 min.
Makes: App. 100 to 150 grams.**

1½ cups soya bean seeds
1 tablespoon Epsom salts (magnesium sulphate)

1. Soak the beans in water for at least 12 hours.
2. Drain all the water and wash the soaked beans.
3. Grind the soaked beans in a blender to a smooth paste using 4 cups of water.
4. Strain to extract the milk.
5. Boil this milk, add the Epsom salts and remove from the flame.
6. Strain the soya bean curd through a muslin cloth placed on a strainer.
7. Press the bean curd and put some weight on it so that all the water is drained out.
8. Remove the weight after a few hours.
9. To store for a longer period, refrigerate in a container filled with water.

Use as required.

☺Paneer is a good substitute for tofu.

PANEER

Paneer is a by-product of milk and is surprisingly easy to make if you follow these simple steps.

**Preparation time: a few minutes.   Cooking time: 10 minutes.
Makes 250 to 300 gms.**

1 litre full cream milk
2 teaspoons lemon juice

1. Put the milk to boil. When it starts boiling, switch off the gas and wait for a while.
2. Add the lemon juice and when it curdles, drain on a muslin cloth.
3. If you want solid paneer, put some weight on the drained paneer and leave it on for some time.
4. Use as required in the recipe.

☀ You can also use vinegar or citric acid crystals instead of lemon juice.

RED CURRY PASTE

Picture on page 54
Preparation time: 10 minutes.   No cooking.   Makes 1 cup.

10 red chillies, soaked in warm water for 10 minutes and drained
1 onion, chopped
4 cloves garlic, peeled
1 tablespoon ginger, grated
2 stalks lemon grass
6 stalks coriander
1 tablespoon ground coriander
2 tablespoons ground cumin
½ teaspoon white pepper
½ teaspoon salt

1. Grind all the ingredients to a paste in a mortar or a food processor using a little water.
2. Store in an airtight container (for upto 1 month). Alternatively, freeze for upto 3 months.
3. Use as required.

☺ To obtain a bright red curry paste, use red Kashmiri chillies as far as possible.

GREEN CURRY PASTE

Picture on page 54

Preparation time: 10 minutes.   No cooking.
Makes 1 cup.

10 green chillies, chopped
6 cloves garlic, peeled
1 onion, chopped
20 mm. (¾") piece of ginger, peeled
1 cup chopped coriander
rind of 1 lemon, grated
juice of ½ lemon
1 tablespoon ground coriander
2 teaspoons ground cumin
2 stalks lemon grass
1 teaspoon salt
½ teaspoon pepper

1. Grind all the ingredients in a mortar or a food processor using a little water.
2. Store in an airtight container or in the refrigerator. Alternatively, freeze for upto 3 months.
3. Use as required.

☼ Make 2 recipes of this paste as you might need it for another recipe, eg. Thai fried rice, Table-top Thai Curry or to use another time when you are in a hurry.